ONE HUNDRED YEARS

JEAN BOVELL

Published by Jean Bovell 2024

Copyright © Jean Bovell 2024

All rights reserved. No part of this publication may be reproduced, stored in a retrieval system, or transmitted in any form or by any means, electronic, mechanical, photocopy, recording or otherwise, without prior written permission of the copyright owner. Nor can it be circulated in any form of binding or cover other than that in which it is published and without similar condition including this condition being imposed on a subsequent purchaser

ISBN:
978-1-915351-36-4

Published by
DolmanScott
www.dolmanscott.co.uk

PROLOGUE

The history of slavery cuts across many cultures, nationalities and religions, from ancient times to the present day. And was in olden days an accepted practice in Europe, Asia, Africa, and the Middle East.

The practice involves the capture of vulnerable individuals who are treated as property and intimidated into a life of servitude by people that a more powerful.

The trans-Atlantic slave trade was the largest slave trade in history, and was in operation from the early 1500s to the 1860s.

It is estimated that during the period, a total of 20 million men, women and children, the vast majority being from Central and West African countries had been transported across the Atlantic.

African slaves were in the majority sold by West African slave traders to Dutch, British, Portugues and Spanish slave traders, in exchange for merchandise such as iron bars, liquor, fire arms, and Cowie Shells, which were at the time, highly valued in various West African countries.

Apart from being an acceptable form of currency, Cowie Shells were also used for making jewellery, hair ornaments and charms, and sewn into classic garments.

In parallel with ongoing trading transactions, individuals were being captured in droves from coastal areas, and like purchased slaves, were shackled and shepherded onto ships.

The enslaved peoples were categorised as cargo to be transported to the Americas as quickly as possible, and subjected to brutal and inhumane treatments.

Over one million lives were consequently lost, during transit.

The resilient individuals who had endured and survived what could be described as a long and punishing passage across the oceans, were on arrival at their destination, sold on to European Planters. And thereafter, coerced into working on cotton, sugar, coffee, tobacco, and cocoa plantations, rice fields, gold, and silver mines, the construction industry, and as domestic servants, within various European colonies in the Caribbean and in Central and South America.

Western economies were at the time being created, boosted, and sustained by the unpaid labour that was being provided by African slaves.

The highly profitable buying and selling of humans which began in the early 16th century, was officially abolished on August 1st 1834.

Based on fact, the story chronicles the different ways in which the enslaved who lived on colonised countries in Central and South America and on Caribbean islands, rebelled against an oppressive regime, and succeeded in establishing independent lives.

It progresses to a post slavery period, when economic opportunities that promised a better life, were being enthusiastically embraced by the liberated peoples of the Caribbean. But centres on the journey of the men who laboured during the American-led construction of the Panama Canal, and the proceeding 100-year long campaign for official accreditation for their invaluable sacrifices.

Although a significant number of labourers on the canal construction originated from islands such as Grenada, Jamaica, St Lucia, St Vincent, and Trinidad and Tobago, most contracted labourers had been recruited from the island of Barbados.

Barbados was the first British Colony to be populated by a black majority.

This retrospective is reinterpreted and delivered in a format that endeavours to capture the spirit and experiences of lives once lived.

Jean Bovell

Acknowledgements

Sincere gratitude to Stephen Lewis for his highly-valued assistance with research, the provision of images, and information contained within the narrative that refers to specific individuals.

Much appreciation extended to Dr Joseph Radix for sharing personal experiences of his trip along the Panama Canal.

Special thanks to Joseph Mackintosh for his expert assistance with technical photography issues.

Factual data obtained from internet searches.

Content:

The Inaugaration Of The Panama Canal 1
The Caribben Of An Era 3
Seduced By The Irresitable Offer Of Lucrative Work 9
The Jamaican Experience 17
The Road Was Long And Hard.. 21
The Enslaved In Panama 24
The Panama Railroads 26
What Next For Unemployed West Indians 28
The Birth Of A Nation.. 30
Golden Expectations.. 32
Rough Transit 34
The American Control Canal Zone 37
The Gold-Roll And Silver-Roll Divide 40
Dashed Hopes 45
A Flourishing Piece Of Nature....................................... 47
Back-Breaking Labour... 50
Critical Consequences... 52
Living The Dream 55

Lights That Shone Through The Darkness 58
Very Important Visitors 62
Hell's Gorge 66
The Finishing 70
Onwards And Upwards 73
Reflections 79
The Unravelling 82
One-Hundred Years Afterwards 84

The Inaugaration Of The Panama Canal

The official opening of the Panama Canal on August 15th 1914 with the passing of the American passenger and cargo Steam Ship, SS Ancon, had been a momentous event in world history. The long-held vision of a man-made waterway through the isthmus of Panama, the narrow strip of land that lay between the Atlantic and Pacific Oceans, had finally become a reality following 10 years of strategic but dangerous operations.

The world was wonderstruck.

At a cost of $352 million dollars, and many thousand lives, it was at that point in time, the most expensive and challenging project that had ever been undertaken and successfully completed.

It symbolised a staggering victory of technology over nature, and was given the accolade, "Eighth Wonder" of the world.

The Engineers who had master-minded the world's first artificial lake that enabled a quicker and cheaper route for transporting cargo, commercial goods, and passengers, between the Atlantic and Pacific Oceans, received world-wide acclaim for their incredible ingenuity.

Due however, to the onset of World War 1, on 28th July 1914, the grand celebrations that had been planned for the inauguration was scaled down but postponed to an undetermined future date. Moreover, the front-pages of newspapers in many countries across the globe were being at the time dominated by revelations of the activities of the war that had been raging across Europe. Consequently, information relating to the official opening of the Panama Canal, failed to make the headlines.

Although the Americans were being rightfully applauded for their technological expertise and economic might, the triumphant completion of the greatest infrastructure the world had ever seen, could not have been realised if it were not for the blood, sweat and grit of the contracted labourers that had been recruited from the British Colonised West Indian islands.

However, their gruelling and high-risk manual involvements were not at the time acknowledged.

The records indicate that of the 75,0000 men that had been contracted from the Caribbean by the American Canal Company for the purpose of carrying out the most laborious and dangerous tasks, approximately 45,000 originated from the island of Barbados.

An estimated total of 20,000 contracted labourers lost their lives and an undisclosed number sustained life-changing injuries during the process of the canal construction.

One-hundred years would elapse before the unheralded heroes of yester-year, are posthumously recognised, and honoured for their gallant and indispensable participations.

The Caribbean Of An Era

During the early years of the 20th century, Edward V11 reigned over the United Kingdom and the British Empire.

Edward V11 ascended the throne after the death of his mother, Queen Victoria, on January 22nd 1901.

The coronation of Edward V11 and Alexandra, as King and Queen of the British Realm, was officiated on August 9th 1902.

Known as the Edwardian era, it was a period when various islands in the Caribbean had been colonised by the British, and an Official, known as a Governor, was appointed to each island.

The Governor represented the British Crown and ensured that United Kingdom laws and statutes were being upheld.

The economy of these majority Christian small island Caribbean states was in those days largely dependent on agriculture, but principally cotton, cocoa, and sugar.

Although generally hard-working, many people were poor and lived simple lives.

Families in rural communities were essentially reliant on produce that had been cultivated and reaped from the land. And were further sustained by the rearing of farm animals such as chickens, cattle, goats, and pigs.

Specific plants or "bush," known for their unique healing properties, were brewed into teas, and ingested for curing common ailments such as fevers, colds, and headache. Moreover, varieties such as Aloe Vera were blended into creams for soothing and healing the various skin conditions that were prevalent at the time.

These tried and tested generational herbal remedies are to the present day considered by various individuals to be safe and effective medicinal alternatives.

The early twentieth century was in the Caribbean, also an age when elementary schooling was accessible to all children, and Secondary education was a fee-paying privilege, and reserved for the children of the "wealthy".

The comparatively "well-to-do" families of the day were likely to have been headed by land-owners, professional practitioners, or skilled workers, most of whom may have resided in urban areas.

These advantaged individuals occupied houses that were large and spacious, built with bricks and concrete, and in most cases, adjoining stables.

Although "automobiles" were at the time in existence, they were unaffordable, even for the people that were deemed to be "rich." And ownership of horses may therefore, have been symbolic of a person's wealth and social standing.

The outer-walls of "palatial" dwellings were painted in bold and bright colours with plush interior furnishings that included gleamingly polished mahogany tables and chairs, and a wicker-seated rocking-chair, which was, at the time, a highly desired possession. Although, the elegant four-poster bed complete with mosquito net, that stood majestically in the master bed-room, may have been the ultimate statement of class and sophistication.

In contrast, many disadvantaged people resided in communities that were located within sleepy rural parishes, and in which there may have been at least one church, a school house, and a small town.

Poor families lived mainly in one-room huts or two-room houses, that were commonly erected by the owner with assistance from relatives and friends, and built with wood but in some cases, a combination of bamboo, mud, and large branches.

Self-constructed humble dwellings of the period contained no plumbing or electricity, and were usually fitted with basic items of wooden furniture that had been made to order by a local carpenter.

Most families in poor rural areas of the age, conducted day-to-day living routines out of doors. It included cooking on coal-pots, baking in stone ovens, and bathing and laundering in rivers and streams. And houses were places where women gave birth, individuals rested when they were feeling unwell, but most importantly where families would enter at dusk, and kneel together in prayer under the glow of lighted candles or oil lamps before bedding down for the night.

It was at the time usual practice, that women from poor communities across the Caribbean, were employed as servants at the homes of those who were financially better-off. And disadvantaged individuals of both sexes were hired to work in the fields. However, due the unsustainable low wage they received for their services, earnings had been supplemented in various innovated ways and involved the selling of freshly caught fish, meat from slaughtered farm animals and bread, buns and puddings that had been baked in large outdoor stone-ovens. Those that were in possession of small-holdings may in addition have profited from produce reaped.

The mode of transport commonly accessible to people in disadvantaged communities of the day, was likely to have been the stubbornly lethargic donkey. Consequently, simply getting around on foot was for most, the preferred and reliably speedier option.

It was, therefore, not uncommon that groups of women, some of whom may have been barefooted, trekked for miles to the nearest large town or city on market days, with large baskets stacked with various edible products perched on their heads.

On arrival, desirable spaces were freely selected and claimed, prior to items for sale being unloaded and attractively displayed. These may have included a colourful selection of fruit and vegetables, as well as various ground produce such as yam and sweet potatoes.

Before too long the lady-vendors from the countryside were being swamped by an army of individuals who lived in nearby urban districts and were reliant on country folk for providing the fresh produce they required.

The prospective buyers never failed to examine and squeeze the desired variety before demanding to know the selling price. "How Much"! "How Much"! they bellowed while jostling to be first served.

However, prices were rarely more than they could afford, and it was guaranteed that within a short period of time, everything for sale would have been "snapped up."

Thereafter, the precious "takings" were carefully tallied prior to being placed in a string purse that was made of cloth and secured within the bosom.

At the end of a financially rewarding day, the female traders from the countryside may have indulged in purchasing a few of the items they required but were not available in their local shops. And may have been material for making garments, or even a pair of much needed foot-wear.

However, the less burdensome walking journey home may have been savoured care-free moments filled with juicy gossip, hearty laughter, and spontaneous bursts of joyous singing.

Cities or large town in different Caribbean islands of the day were mostly located in coastal areas.

They were comparatively bustling centres in which stood various Government buildings, banks, retail outlets, and a significant place of worship such as a Cathedral. And markets with stalls that provided not only fruit and vegetables, but also freshly prepared meals, snacks, and a variety home-made beverage.

It was, essentially, an open area where women donned in hats or turbans, and dressed in various designs of self-made but largely full-length garments with deep pockets, casually attired men in hats, and boys and girls, some of whom may have been in ragged clothing and barefooted, ambled alongside one another, in atmosphere filled with noises emitted from human chatter and the pounding sounds of riders on horses and horse-driven carriages that galloped along the surrounding narrow streets.

Seduced By The Irresistable Offer Of Work

The American-Led construction of the Panama Canal was initially brought to the attention of Populations across the British Colonised West Indian islands by the American Canal Company in 1905.

The Canal Company had at the time established a labour recruitment station in Bridge Town, Barbados. In conjunction, advertisements listing the different skilled and unskilled jobs that were available to both men and women between the ages of 18 and 40, appeared in newspapers not only in Barbados but also various islands within the region. Importantly, able-bodied young men were urgently needed for carrying-out heavy manual tasks on the ground. And were being offered contracts that incorporated cost-free transit to the Canal Zone, lucrative wages, and benefits that included rent-free accommodation, and cost-free meals and medical care.

The attractive work package arrived at a time in the Caribbean when unemployment among the unskilled was high, and those who had been fortunate to be in work, were being paid very little. And survival within materially dis-advantaged communities had been a day-to-day struggle.

For many who lived on or below the poverty line, the "out of the blue" opening may have been perceived to be an escape route from the "poverty trap," and considered "God Send." While those from "better off" communities, seized the opportunity that promised to increase their wealth.

Not surprisingly, skilled, as well as unskilled individuals across the divide who were not within the stipulated age range, had been tempted to adjust their dates of birth for the purpose of obtaining work on the Canal construction.

An individual who had allegedly deducted several years from his real his age, and was thereafter successful in his application for a non-contract clerical position with the American Canal Company, was known to have been James Mitchell from the island of Grenada.

Mitchell was one of many economic migrants for whom the gamble taken to falsify his personal details resulted in huge dividends. He was said to have received a satisfactory wage for his services, and that he went on to realise his dream by securing a better financial future for his family.

In parallel with the official recruitment drive, the men of Barbados and nearby islands were being further seduced into applying for labouring jobs by a particular impressively dressed individual whose image regularly appeared in the local press.

He was given the nickname "Panama Man."

The young man who was reported to have hailed from humble beginnings, had allegedly returned to the homeland after making a fortune from money earned during his employment as a contracted labourer on the American-led Canal construction.

News of the local boy who had made good in Panama, offered hope to numerous individuals in Barbados and beyond. They were buoyed in the belief that there was a real possibility that they too could be lucratively employed.

The carrot being dangled by the so called "Panama Man" was for most, overwhelmingly enticing.

The celebrity returnee was alleged to have been in person easily recognizable, and stood out from the crowd, as he swaggered along narrow streets in the city of Bridgetown Barbados, puffing on a fat cigar.

He was reported to have "cut a dash" dressed in a tailored white suit, matching shirt, and tie, and eye-catching Panama hat.

The Panama man did not, allegedly, hesitate to pause and acknowledge passers-by, by tipping his hat with a hand that was adorned with thick gold rings, and flashing a smile that displayed strategically placed gold teeth. Moreover, he was reported to have been observed withdrawing large amounts of American gold coins from his pockets.

It had been, for the wide-eyed witnesses, who had never seen such vast sums of money, a breath-taking "pinch me" moment in time. And before too long, glorified stories of the man who had made his fortune from working as a contracted labourer on the Canal construction were being spread throughout Barbados and neighbouring islands, by those who had been in his presence, and others who ran with the story, and passed on to others their unique fanciful or embellished versions.

For those born and raised in materially impoverished Caribbean communities of the day, money, denoted success. And individuals who had worked hard and may have succeeded in accumulating relatively substantial amounts of cash, were on a whole, role models, and highly respected.

The Panama Man had been for most, the manifestation of the things that were achievable. And there was consensus in the belief that even what had been considered the impossible dream, could come true.

The impressionable young West Indians of the period may not have questioned whether the message they were receiving from the magnetic "Panama Man" was genuine, or a charade, intended to bring about a particular desired outcome.

The truth of the matter was yet to be revealed.

However, there could be no doubting that the number of people seeking both contract and non-contract employment within the Canal Zone in anticipation of accumulating wealth, increased significantly as a direct result of the appearance of the mesmerising and persuasive "Panama Man."

The American Recruitment Centre, stationed in Barbados, and agents based on islands such as Dominica, Grenada, St Lucia, St Vicent, and Trinidad and Tobago, were being swamped daily, by individuals applying for work on the Canal construction.

Despite most applications being from young men seeking employment as contracted labourers, men as well as women were at the same time, independently applying for other jobs that were available to both skilled and unskilled Caribbean workers. These included drivers, domestics, carpenters, masons, administrators, health care workers, and teachers.

A fair number of workers from the French Colonies of Martinique and Guadeloupe were in tangent being recruited from an American Canal Agency that had been based on the island of Martinique.

Panama had "opened-up," and an entire generation was being swept into the wave of excitement and optimism that was at the time cascading throughout the small island nations of the Caribbean.

The chance of a better life had been fully embraced by individuals across all communities. And included skilled workers who earned a relatively high wage, and belonged to better-off communities.

Although the irresistible offers of work on an unprecedented waterway that was being built in an exotic faraway land had been enthusiastically received by most, there were nonetheless those who remained unwavering in their decision to "stay put." They may have consisted of individuals who received a fair wage and were largely satisfied with their living and working circumstances, and desired no more. Those who suspected that the glowing promises could not be true because they sounded too good. While others simply did not wish to relocate to a foreign country and were resigned to living the simple life. It was, after all, all they ever knew.

Despite being materially deprived, families in poor areas had been for the most part, secure in their surroundings. And the collective sense of belonging that prevailed, may have been derived from being members of a community that was both caring and sharing. And where the children were required to participate in the daily survival routines, such as reaping crop, fetching water from streams and springs, looking after the animals, and fishing in the surrounding seas.

The people who lived off the land and looked after each other, rarely experienced gnawing hunger, or feelings of loneliness. But even though they might not have been particularly mindful or appreciative of these fundamental riches, they were being spiritually strengthened by their Christian beliefs. And in some cases, reassured by long held superstitions and associated rituals that had been passed down generational lines.

Furthermore, everyone looked forward to participating in social events, such as the annual harvest festival, or cultural land-mark celebrations that may have involved costume dressing, music, dance, and plenty of eating and drinking. Competitive cricket was also popular in the region of the period, and attracted huge numbers of spectators.

The life routines that were being conducted daily, did not, however, preclude the fact that women of the age were largely subservient to their men folk. While on the other hand, and regardless of being married, single or co-habiting with a female, too many men assumed that it had been their God-given right to be promiscuous. And consequently, unashamedly conducted affairs and impregnated females in communities up and down the various islands.

It was the case, nonetheless, that most Caribbeans of the era, aspired lucratively productive lives that would ensure better education and career opportunities for themselves and their family. Consequently, the surprise offer of well-paid work in Panama that was guaranteed to transform lives, had been wholeheartedly embraced.

A golden opportunity had suddenly appeared on the horizon and thousands would rush towards it.

Additionally, the idea of being enabled to set foot on the Republic of Panama, which was at the time perceived by many West Indians to be an exotic Spanish speaking nation, somewhere on the continent of South America, may have been an intoxicating prospect for many.

Even youngsters were being swept into the feverish feel-good buzz that was sweeping across the region, and would speak excitedly of a parent or close relative who had signed-up for work on the canal construction.

In a climate that was essentially euphorically optimistic, newspaper editorials that warned of the harsh realities and racial inequalities that existed within the American control Canal Zone, were being largely ignored.

It is indicated on historical records that by the end of 1905, 19,900 fit young men between the ages 18 and 40 of Barbadian origin were contracted to work on the construction of the Panama Canal, and at that point accounted for 70% of the total West Indian workforce. The remaining 30% had been contracted from islands that included Grenada, Jamaica, Martinique, St Lucia, and Trinidad and Tobago.

Although the response to recruitment drives that was ongoing in the Eastern Caribbean and neighbouring islands, exceeded expectation, similar campaigns that had been initiated on the island of Jamaica had been less successful.

The Jamaican Experience

History informs that most of the Labourers on the French-led Canal construction had been recruited from the British colonised island of Jamaica.

Jamaica lies in the Atlantic Ocean and in a location that is adjacent to the isthmus of Panama.

At the time of the American-led construction, efforts had been initially made at recruiting labourers from China. However, the Chinese who were reputed to be hardworking and reliable, showed little interest in taking up the offer of work, and subsequent campaigns carried out in Spain, Italy, and Greece, also received negligible response.

The recruitment of many thousands of labourers, essentially for undertaking the fundamental task of clearing the vast and untamed terrain in preparation for the proposed construction of a canal, had been paramount. Consequently, the American Canal company was at that point left with little option but to switch their recruitment drive to the English-speaking West Indian Islands.

In those days, the deeply held stereotypical view that "all black men were lazy, stupid and worthless" persisted.

And may have been the primary reason for which the "last stance" decision was allegedly reluctantly taken.

Despite the ingrained negative assumptions, there could have been no denying that many prospered from the free labour of slaves. Moreover, men from the region and particularly those from the island of Jamaica, had been reputed not only for their willingness to seize any opportunity of work that came their way after slavery was officially abolished, but their high levels of resilience, and physical capacity for undertaking hard labour, had been proven.

Historical records indicate that most of the labourers on the French-led canal construction which began in 1882 and ended in 1889, had been enlisted from the British Colonised Island of Jamaica.

It may have been the basis on which Jamaica was at first targeted by the American Canal Company.

Despite these factors, Jamaica's response to American recruitment endeavours did not have the desired outcome.

Relatively few young Jamaican males who met the physical and mental requirements, showed enthusiasm or willingness to accept the offer of "well-paid" work on the American-led canal construction.

The general malaise exhibited by the Jamaicans of the era, may have been related to collective feelings of weariness, and mistrust, that stemmed from historical accounts of the harrowing experiences of a generation of Jamaican-born men who perished, or sustained life-altering injuries, while working on the French-led Canal construction.

Prior to embarking on the mammoth task of constructing a canal across the isthmus of Panama, the French had master-minded the building of a waterway, at sea level, in Egypt, that connects the Mediterranean Sea and the Red Sea. The construction started on 25th April 1859 and was successfully completed on 17th November 1869. It is known as the Suez Canal.

It is documented that at the beginning of French-led operations in the isthmus of Panama, 10,844 Caribbean labourers were recorded on the French pay-roll. Of these, 9005, were Jamaican, and a combined total of 1,839 workers had been recruited from Barbados, Grenada, Martinique, and Trinidad and Tobago.

An additional 15,000 men were subsequently being recruited from the island of Jamaica on an annual basis. And accounted for 90% of the overall labour-force.

Approximately 22,000 Jamaican lives had been lost due to accidents, suicide and diseases that included malaria and yellow fever. And an indeterminate number of individuals was alleged to have sustained life-changing injury.

The French-led attempt at constructing a waterway across the isthmus of Panama commenced on January 20th 1882. The seemingly insurmountably dangerous and costly operation was unexpectedly and abruptly abandoned on February 4th 1889.

The redundant Jamaican labourers received no financial remuneration, and while many of the almost penniless individuals returned home, others went on to find alternative employment on plantations in Central and

South America, and at a later stage, may have been joined by spouses and close family members.

The Road Was Long And Hard

Pursuant to legislation passed by the British Government in 1833 in relation to the Trans-Atlantic slavery trade, Slavery was officially abolished in British Colonial West Indian Islands on 1st August 1834.

Upon being informed of the long sought after and life-changing announcement that had been finally released after centuries of being held in bondage, freed slaves across the region, as well as their supporters would have undoubtedly been joyously ecstatic.

The historical and jubilant moment came after many years of organised rebellion and insurrection by the enslaved against domination and exploitation.

The enduring offensives that had been mounted by Caribbean slaves during the eighteenth and nineteenth centuries, included Jacky's rebellion on the island of Jamaica in the 1760s, the Haitian uprising of 1789, Fedon's revolution on the island of Grenada in 1790s, the Bussa led slave revolt in Barbados that occurred in 1816 and resulted in a quarter of the island's sugar crop being extinguished by fire before the rebellion had been eventually supressed. The Demerara revolt in British Guyana in 1823, and the Jamaican slave uprising of 1831.

Similar rebellious action had also taken place on the islands of Dominica and St Lucia, during the period.

Although each insurrection had been quickly quelled, spirits were never broken and the burning desire for freedom remained unwavering.

The on-going campaign against the repressive regime included organised protests, and ambush, or terrorist style attacks against individual oppressors.

Despite the initial euphoric reaction to the termination of the Trans-Atlantic slave trade, many liberated slaves were not freed from the trappings of subjugation.

Financial compensation had not been placed on the table, and they were therefore reliant on the good-will of European Planters for opening a door that would lead to true independence.

The so called "lucky" families who had been given a helping hand towards a new start in life by being gifted small plots of land, achieved autonomy by growing their own crop, and profiting from selling surpluses at market.

Those who were less fortunate had been left with little choice but to continue in servitude.

Although free labour was under Abolition Statutes, unlawful, freed slaves who remained in the service of Planters, were being paid an unsustainable minimum wage. Consequently, aspiring individuals who desired self-sufficiency struggled to accumulate the downpayment required for purchasing by instalments, even the smallest piece of land that was at the time necessary for enabling a way forward.

Despite the disparities that related to employment, self-determination was nonetheless being collectively achieved within post slavery communities. These were spaces in which individuals were being respected, valued, and empowered to contribute constructively, towards the development of the then new but uniquely different Caribbean societies.

The economy of the Caribbean islands of the period had been crucially dependent on the production of Sugar. Consequently, following the unexpected drop in the global price of sugar, many freed peoples, and particularly those who had been solely reliant on menial earnings, craved financial security and an altogether better life.

They would, therefore, enthusiastically sign-up for the better-paid manual work that were being offered on foreign soil.

The Enslaved In Panama

Most people who resided on British colonised West Indian islands of the period, may have heard of Panama, and specifically a country that located somewhere within the continent of South America. Very few, however, would have been aware that Panama was also historically a participant in the Trans-Atlantic slave trade.

It is documented that during the colonial era, large numbers of people were being continually captured or purchased from various countries in West Africa, and transported to Panama for the specific purpose of loading and unloading vessels, carrying goods across the isthmus, and for working on various plantations and goldmines.

Directions relating to working requirements were not however at all times observed, and were at various times unexpectedly and uncharacteristically received with non-compliance by defiant slaves who acted by fleeing the autocratic environment.

As far back as 1531, a series of organised escapes resulted in thousands of Panamanian slaves retreating to remote jungle areas in Eastern Panama.

They may have been experienced in developing strategies for surviving in the wild, such as the ability to make basic tools, and light fires from natural resources. But it is likely that escapees were being sustained by various edible products obtained from the surrounding forests, and by hunting for and capturing birds and wild animals. Moreover, Large branches and barks cut from the trunks and branches of trees were probably used for constructing basic shelters.

Despite the precarious beginnings, the descendants of runaway slaves would in the passage of time establish self-governing communities, and evolve into becoming nationalised Afro-Panamanians.

The runaway slaves of Panama were commonly known as "Cimarrons" (Wild Ones).

It was the term from which "Maroon" had been derived and used to define runaway slaves from British Colonised Caribbean islands.

The Panama Railroads

The construction of rail-roads across the isthmus of Panama linking the Atlantic Ocean to the Pacific Ocean, was reportedly the vision of a group of business men from New York.

The building proposal was consolidated by the formation of the American Railroad Company, and permission for initiating the project was thereafter granted by the Governing Body of the Republic of New Granada.

The Republic of New Granada was at the time a Spanish colonised group of countries that incorporated Columbia, Panama, and specific small areas in Brazil, Costa Rica, Ecuador, Peru, and Venezuela.

The different skilled and unskilled workers required for the major undertaking had been recruited from far away countries, and included China, England, Germany, India, and Ireland. Although individuals who resided on nearby British colonised West Indian islands were being first and foremost targeted.

The offer of a reasonable wage for services rendered had been immediately and comprehensively welcomed by a people who had not too long previously, achieved freedom, and desired the finance that would enable a better quality of life.

The construction of the Panama-railroads began in 1850 and ended in 1855.

Upon completion in 1855, the newly built railroads, estimated to be over 47 miles long, resulted in an expedite train service that transported people as well as merchandise, to and from the Atlantic Ocean and across the isthmus of Panama. And moreover, reduced significantly, the time taken to travel between the East Coast to the West Coast of the United States of America.

The Panama Rail-roads was at the time of completion, proclaimed an outstanding engineering achievement, and was globally applauded for being the first trans-continental rail-road in the world.

It could not have been anticipated back then, that the Panama Railroads would at some point in the future prove integral to the success of yet another unprecedented American-led endeavour.

What Next For Unemployed West Indians

After the completion of the Panama railroads, a fair number of redundant Caribbeans would return to their respective homeland and savings accrued from working on the Railroads, may have been used for improving living standards.

Due, however, to the resurgence in the demand for sugar which coincided with the completion of Railroads construction, large numbers of individuals chose to embark on yet another lucrative adventure. And pursued employment that was now available on revitalised Sugar Plantations in Cuba, Central America, and the United States.

Caribbean railroad workers who had taken the decision to remain in Panama would go on to find alternative employment, and after settling into their new lives, welcomed being joined by loved ones who had been left behind.

West Indian immigrants in Panama, settled in an area known as Bocas del Toro and in the course of time became self-sufficient from farming small holdings. And thereafter, broadened their horizons further, by pioneering the cultivation of large crops of bananas for the specific purpose of selling to American Wholesalers.

Consequent to the continual high demand for bananas from retailers in North, Central and South America, what had begun as a small business venture, developed into a large and immensely profitable enterprise.

The highly successful wholesale business was sometime later adopted by American wholesalers. And resulted in banana plantations being established by the United States Fruit Company at various locations in Nicaragua, Honduras, and Costa Rica.

Due to their experience and overall expertise in the planting and harvesting of banana crop, farm workers from the Caribbean were specifically targeted for working on American-owned plantations.

The practice remained in place throughout the early years of the 20th century.

The Birth Of A Nation

The Isthmus of Panama is the ten-mile strip of land in Panama that connects Central America to South America.

It is situated between the Atlantic Ocean and the Pacific Ocean.

Panama was originally a small province of Columbia and part of the colony known as New Granada that had been established by the Spanish in 1538.

New Granada achieved Independence from Spain in 1886.

Panama broke away from Columbia following an American-backed rebel-led bloodless coup that lasted just a few hours. It resulted in the birth of the Republic of Panama on 3rd November 1903.

The newly declared independent nation was recognised by the United States three days subsequently on 6th November 1903.

Columbian troops who had been in combat with the rebels were paid off by the United States Government to retreat from the country.

A treaty granting the Americans use of the Isthmus for constructing an artificial waterway in exchange for financial compensation was thereafter agreed and signed.

Panama was at that point in time a Spanish-speaking Roman Catholic country. The majority population was Mestizos.

Mestizos are a people of mixed Amerindian, African and European heritage.

Panama was in those days a sleepy tropical country and comprised of small close-knit communities.

The land consisted of rich and fertile soil and yielded an abundant variety of produce. These included sugar-cane, coco-beans, coco-nuts, rice and maize, and tropical fruit such as bananas, pineapples, water-melons, and oranges.

Golden Expectations

Fortune seekers from Barbados and other English-speaking West Indian islands such as Trinidad, St Lucia, and Grenada, who responded to the offer of lucratively paid employment in the American control Canal Zone may have been consumed with eager anticipation, and anxious to set off on the journey that would take them to the "Promise Land."

Ships commissioned by the American Canal for carrying contract workers to the isthmus free of cost, departed from a port in Barbados on a fortnightly basis. However, it was common knowledge that non-contract economic migrants who were unable to afford the price of a ticket to the isthmus, were being permitted free transit. And it was often the case that individuals from different islands hopped on vessels for the short trip to Barbados with the view of securing a cost-free journey to the isthmus.

People from the various islands who were able to meet the $14 asking price of a ticket, were required to board one of the boats that departed from a named port on the island of Trinidad to the isthmus on regular fortnightly schedules.

Although levels of expectation and positivity among contract and non-contracted Caribbean migrant workers were of equal measure, individuals on fee-paying vessels to the Zone journeyed in conditions that were relatively satisfactory, while others who travelled free of charge, endured an altogether hellish transit.

Rough Transit

The provision of free passage to the isthmus of Panama was enthusiastically welcomed not only by contracted labourers but also by those with limited financial resources who had chosen to be independent in their search for a better life.

Any optimistic expectation that non-paying passengers may have harboured regarding their trip across the seas had been unceremoniously dashed on discovering that they were being herded like cattle onto the deck of ships, and informed that they were required to remain there for the entire journey.

The space designated to non-paying passengers had been essentially, no more than the ground they stood on. And their entitlement to food and fluids had been limited.

Although individuals with personal supplies of sustenance may have been willing to share them with others, most free-travelling passengers may have experienced gnawing hunger and associated digestion issues throughout the journey.

Consequently, a tensed and stress-filled atmosphere, fuelled by insufficient nutrients and mobility restrictions had taken hold. And resulted in fragile tempers, heated arguments and fist-fights, that was often being triggered by trivial mis-understandings between men with rumbling stomachs and aching limbs.

These "classless" and mis-treated non-paying passengers were during the period, commonly known as "Deckers."

Although the endurance of "Deckers" had been tested, the collective underlying feelings of hope and positivity remained undiminished. Therefore, despite being both exhausted and relieved to be disembarking their ship at the end of what could have been described as a long and almost intolerable journey, "Deckers" were buoyant in the belief that they had stepped onto the path that promised to lead to prosperity.

At the journey's end, and after weeks of discomfort and being fed a meagre diet, the men had been anxious to get their teeth into a substantial portion of "food" followed by a good night's sleep on a longed-for comfortable bed. They had after-all signed Contract Agreements that incorporated the provision of furnished accommodation and nutritious meals.

However, as they were being transported to their place of residence, new arrivals of contracted labourers to the Canal Zone, could not have imagined that they were about to enter a living and working environment that was harsh and merciless. And that their rosy expectations would soon be shattered.

The experiences of arrivals of fortune-seekers who travelled independently had been, on the other hand, quite different to that of their contracted counterparts.

Although large numbers of non-contract migrants would most likely have been greeted by relatives or friends who had already settled into working lives in the Zone, those without connections may have received assistance with navigating a way forward.

However, even though most independent migrants had secured some form of skilled or unskilled employment with the American Canal Company prior to entering the Zone, unaccompanied unskilled female migrants, were largely employed as domestics at the homes of Gold-rollers. Cooks, kitchen-hands and servers in bars and restaurants, and chamber maids, launderers, and cleaners in hotels.

Non-contract workers from the Caribbean were essentially self-reliant and would come together in building small communities that were reflective of cultural norms.

The American Controlled Canal Zone

After becoming a Republic in 1903, Panama granted the United States Government, the use, occupation, and control of the isthmus and land-underwater. It was to be used primarily for the construction, maintenance, operation, and protection of a waterway, across the isthmus, in return for an agreed annual fee.

The newly acquired territory was opened officially on 4th May 1904. And was thereafter known as the American-controlled Canal Zone.

The region was divided into two administrative sub-division districts called the Balboa Heights and Cristobel.

The Balboa Heights was located near to the Pacific Ocean, and was the area in which the Administrative Headquarters of the Canal Zone Government and the Panama Canal Company had been based.

The province known as Cristobel bordered the Atlantic Ocean.

The construction of the Panama Canal began on 4th May 1904.

By the year, 1905, most of the canal employees that had been recruited from the United States, fled the Zone in large numbers. They were in fear of contracting one of the deadly infectious diseases that were at the time rampant within the Zone.

The most dreaded of these was Yellow Fever, an extremely painful and debilitating condition that was very often fatal.

Following the discovery that mosquitos had been largely responsible for the spread of the disease, appropriate measures for ridding the territory of these particularly harmful insects were initiated.

The process involved the spraying of a mixture of kerosene and crude oil over mosquito lava in all water sources, including puddles. Covers were placed over water systems, and all buildings were fumigated. The methodical undertaking was largely successful, and by the beginning of 1906, there was a significant reduction in the number of reported yellow fever cases.

In parallel with the action that was taken for controlling lethal infections, the Canal Zone was being developed and transformed into a city that would reflect the affluent lifestyles of the then modern America.

It followed that within a relatively short period of time and as far back as 1908, new-build homes on well-maintained lawns had emerged on pristine tree lined streets. And supportive resources such as schools, churches, hospitals, hotels, and sporting, entertainment, and shopping facilities, had been established. In addition, English was imposed on the territory. And replaced Spanish by being the officially recognised primary language within the American controlled Canal Zone.

The indigenous cultural norms of the what was previously a Spanish colony had been essentially cancelled, rebuilt, and contrived to emulate American traditions, expectations, values, language, and overall way-of-life.

The up-grading of living standards did not, however, extend to all areas within the Zone.

In contrast to the fully plumbed and electricity wired new build homes in leafy residential areas and alongside brightly paved roads, hundreds of ancient rundown shacks, and barracks stood neglected on dirt roads in remote and gloomy locations.

The abandoned and dilapidated wooden structures with outdoor latrines, and strategically placed water-pipes, had been erected during the time of French-led canal operations that began in 1882 and ended in 1889.

The Gold-Roll And Silver-Roll Divide

Individuals recruited from the Caribbean by the American Canal Company, regardless of employment status, may have not have known the meaning of the words "Silver-roll" that was printed on the top of their employment Agreement forms.

However, they would be awoken to its significance after arriving in the Zone, and discovering that separate Gold-roll and Silver-roll signs pointed to different entrances in communal spaces. It included libraries, recreation facilities, restrooms, drinking fountains and transportation, and the races were in no doubt which were for their use only.

Although Americans of the period alleged that the "Gold-roll" and "Silver-roll" terms had been established by the French, it was nonetheless under the Americans that the labels were being used for determining a person's race and ranking.

Significantly, the Gold-roll and Silver-roll labels had been used for denoting an unequal "payroll" system. And under which, the salaries of white employees or Gold-rollers, were being paid in American gold coins, while the wages of skilled as well as unskilled Silver-rollers consisted of Panamanian silver coins, known as balboas.

During the period of the Canal construction, American gold currency was highly valued, whilst the Panamanian balboas, had been of little worth.

Most Gold-rollers occupied skilled positions. And were deemed deserving of the attractive perks and incentives that were being provided for procuring and retaining their services.

The benefits offered to gold-rollers, included rent free new build homes that were spacious, fully fitted and attractively furnished and decorated. Substantial salaries with entitlement to forty-two days paid holiday each year, an annual minimum of 30 days sick-pay, and purchase discounts on essentials such as food and clothing. Moreover, the stay-at-home wives of gold-roller workers received financial benefits that were being paid on a regular basis.

Gold-roller employees who were single or unaccompanied were placed in the best hotels, and in addition granted the services of a maid for tending to their separate personal requirements.

The meals provided to gold-rollers were served in lush dining halls that contained tables that were surrounded by cushioned chairs, and laid with polished silver cutlery. And menus listed a variety of delicious and nutritional meals that were free of charge.

The various other privileges that were exclusive to gold-rollers included access to entertainment and sporting venues such as bowling alleys, swimming pools, restaurants, bars, and social clubs. Prompt and superior medical attention and care, and a first-class education delivered by highly qualified educators, to their children.

Regardless of whether they were skilled or unskilled, contracted, or non-contracted, workers recruited from the Caribbean were being categorised silver-rollers, and consequently, undeserving of work-related perks or incentives.

The men who had been contracted to carry out the most dangerous tasks were placed at the bottom of the silver-roller pay-scale and received a minimum wage of just 10 Panamanian cents an hour. They were furthermore denied entitlement to sick pay, and annual holidays, and forbidden from entering sporting and entertainment venues.

The rent-free accommodation allocated to low-ranking contracted labourers had been the run-down windowless ancient shacks and barracks that stood abandoned in remote areas.

The rooms in which at least twelve workers were being at any one time accommodated, contained nothing but three-tier bunk-beds that had been jammed against all four walls, and were essentially, unventilated cramped spaces that did not enable a person's privacy or sense of dignity.

Moreover, labourers were not being protected in their dilapidated homes, from the climatic effects of Panama's extreme weather patterns.

They were unable to escape being dampened in their beds from the rain that seeped through leaking roofs throughout the wet season, or alternatively, in the dry season, being desperately in need of a "little breeze" during hot and humid nights.

Meals accessible to contracted labourers, were separately prepared and served in places that were called "Mess Rooms."

These eating facilities contained no tables or chairs. There were no menus or available choices, and meals were basic, bland, and lacked nutritional value. Most disappointingly, portions were small and insufficient for satisfying the stomachs of men that were both famished and exhausted at the end of a long hard-working day.

Although medical consultation had been accessible to contracted labourers, the treatments they received had been inadequate and therefore, largely ineffective.

The exclusion policy that was being operated in the Canal Zone at the time of the American led construction appeared reflective of the Jim Crow statutes.

The Jim Crow laws were passed in the Southern States of America after the abolition of slavery. The regulations enforced the segregation of the races in public places, and denied black people the right to equal opportunity.

Jim Crow laws were enacted between 1877 and 1950.

Despite the divisions, the American Canal Zone was overall, a newly developed dynamic city where businesses boomed and employment was abundant.

It had been the place where skilled and unskilled individuals from across the globe gathered and contributed their separate expertise towards the collaborative effort that was necessary for constructing an unprecedented waterway across the isthmus of Panama.

However, while the privileged gold-rollers donned impressionable Panama hats and puffed on cigars as they swaggered in a bubble of entitlement and pleasure, the disadvantaged and particularly, contracted labourers at the bottom of the heap, grappled with inescapable daily challenges.

Despite the racial divisions, self-reliant silver-roller migrants on the other hand, would waste little time in establishing a comfortable and supportive living environment that was built on a platform of friendship groups and organised social and sporting activities.

Dashed Hopes

The optimistic hopes and expectations of West Indian labourers contracted to the American Canal Company had undoubtedly been dashed on being faced with the reality of the grim conditions under which they were being required to live and work.

The situation was found to be far removed from the glossy advertisements that guaranteed excellent pay and working conditions, and in tangent bolstered by glowing revelations from the successful and highly persuasive "Panama Man" who claimed to have achieved riches from working on the Canal construction.

Many of the now disillusioned souls may have seriously considered the idea of simply "throwing in the towel" and making a hasty retreat. However, after much thought and deliberation, most contracted labourers would decide to stay.

The near unanimous decision to carry-on was most likely based on the reality that any money earned from working on the construction would be significantly more than what they could hope for, back home. But most importantly, sufficient for bettering the lives of loved ones left behind.

In those days, unskilled jobs in British Colonised Caribbean islands were at best, hard to find, and the rate of pay offered to manual workers was at best, minimal.

It was, therefore, "fait accompli" Turning back, had been for most, not the solution.

Contracted labourers who were unable to overcome the depressingly sinking feelings or the worrying sense of foreboding regarding the suspected hardships that lay ahead, may also have pondered on the forewarnings that had been featured in their local press, before arriving at their regrettable but final decision.

The sceptical individuals who decided to prioritise their personal safety and wellbeing, would cut their losses, and break their contracts by simply hurrying to catch the first available vessel for the return journey home.

Independent workers from the Caribbean, for whom the disadvantages of being categorised silver-rollers had been less impactful, did not doubt their decision to live and work in the Canal Zone. However, they could not have imagined the full extent of the difficulties that was being experienced by labourers who had been contracted to the American Canal Company.

A Flourishing Piece Of Nature

The territory identified as being most appropriate for constructing a water-way had been the fifty-mile mountainous stretch of untamed forest that bridged the Atlantic and Pacific oceans.

The area, at that point, appeared as a mystical blanket of greenery. It contained innumerable close growing tall palms, ancient fruit bearing trees, multitude long grass and networks of wayward and entwined shrubs, bushes, and weeds. And was being fragranced by a combination of sweet, woody, and rancid aromas.

This tranquil but unruly and tumultuous piece of nature, had been inhabited by multitudes of diverse species of wild-life creatures.

These included tropical birds with wings that flapped and resounded across the terrain as they flew rapidly and repeatedly in forever changing directions, hopped through the bushes, and feasted on hanging fruit, chirped sweetly, or perched quietly on nests while patiently awaiting the arrival of new born chicks.

All the while different groups of sprightly monkeys may have screeched lustily as they swung across the trees. Or paused on sturdy branches while carefully peeling and munching contentedly on picked fruit that may have included bananas and oranges.

Incorporated into the chaotic jungle chatter may also have been the incessant buzzing and zizzing of crickets and insects. The contrasting sounds of high-and low-pitched expressions of the various four-legged mammals that prowled through the bush in their never-ending search for food. The swishing and whizzing of the smaller varieties that scurried in the undergrowth. The droning of raging rivers and fast flowing streams. And the thumping sounds of torrential rain, howling winds, roaring thunder, and cracking lightening that was almost continuous during the rainy season.

The less vociferous varieties which also claimed a rightful space within the vast terrain may have included brightly coloured butterflies resting on bushes, venomous snakes slithering insidiously between the undergrowth, allegators in mosquito infested bottomless swamps, and frogs and snails that lingered alongside grasslands, and watery mangroves.

This massive area of untouched territory had been particularly susceptible to the extremities of Panama's weather patterns. And was consequently, scorchingly hot and densely humid with temperatures exceeding 120 Fahrenheit or 48 Celsius during the dry season. Or alternatively dogged by torrential rain, strong winds, and frequent thunderous storms, floods, and land-slides throughout the nine-month long rainy season.

The location identified for the building of a man-made waterway, was at the time, a disorderly but thriving habitat of wildlife. And as decreed by "mother nature" a place in which a diverse array of animal and plant populations freely and spontaneously went about the daily business of survival, and were being instinctively procreative.

This fragrant, clamorous, inter-dependent, and enduring natural universe, that was being sustained by climatic elements and nature's resources, would not be easily conquered.

Back-Breaking Labour

The demolishment of the longstanding chaotic but flourishing piece of nature on which the proposed waterway would be constructed had been the initial challenge tasked to labourers.

The laborious operation had been fraught with danger, but it was amid sounds of clanging tools and blunt thuds, and from dawn to dusk on each day of every week, as many as six thousand labourers at any one-time, wielded machetes, spades, axes, picks, and shovels as they proceeded with ridding the seemingly impenetrable forest of its clutter of trees and entangled wild-growing plants.

The men pressed on with the work in hand, despite being battered by strong winds and heavy rain beating on their backs during the rainy season. Or while sweating profusely and uncontrollably in the searingly hot sunshine that persisted throughout the dry season.

Added to their woes, labourers were at the same time having to deal with constant defensive hostilities being mounted against them by the various inhabitants of the vast jungle. It included being besieged and repeatedly stung by swarms of insects that buzzed noisily and annoyingly around their heads and faces, confronted by, and painfully wounded by barking animals, savaged by flocks of stampeding birds, and all the while being continually fearful of falling victim to one or more of the deadly snakes that were suspected to be wriggling unobtrusively somewhere within the bushes.

Of the different venomous snakes that infested the terrain, most feared was the 10-foot long Mapana whose venom attacked the nervous system, and resulted in internal bleeding and organ degeneration.

Although the clothing worn by labourers such as wide-brimmed straw hats, long-sleeve upper garments and knee-high boots would have provided a degree of protection, they were not being effectively safeguarded from the flurry of never-ending aggressive responses that were being sparked by the ongoing destructive directives. It was nonetheless with unwavering focus, vigour, and enduring stamina, that contracted labourers tackled gruelling tasks.

It seemed that this generation of young men from the Caribbean had unwittingly entered a place that could have been likened to a "war zone."

They were being attacked with belligerence from various fronts in their war with nature. And like soldiers on the front-line of any war, they would pay the ultimate price.

Critical Consequences

The scale and severity of the resistance that was being mounted against labourers by the different species of wild-life and by the forces of nature, resulted in countless casualties.

Large numbers of men were not only having to cope with broken bones and painful and inflamed wounds that resulted mainly from accidents or animal inflictions, many also fell victim to the various contagious diseases, such as malaria, typhoid, and yellow fever, which caused vomiting and bleeding gums, and was at the time, out of control within the Zone.

Exposure to extreme and diverse weather patterns, moreover, impacted the health and wellbeing of labourers. And cases of pneumonia, bronchitis, coughs and colds during the Wet Season, or dehydration and heat-stroke in the Dry Season, had been numerous.

Added to the labourer's tribulations, had been the prevalence of debilitating conditions such as malnutrition, dysentery, and chronic fatigue, which had been due essentially to poor dietary intake.

Although many of those who had been stricken with one or more of the contagious diseases may have harboured expectations of a full recovery, there was no such hope for the unfortunate individuals who had been bitten by the Mapana snake. And in all cases experienced an excruciatingly painful death that very often occurred on a hospital ward that delivered sub-standard medical care.

Despite being denied the treatments that were necessary for curing serious illness, contracted labourers, like every other category of workers, had nonetheless been entitled to receive "Quinine" free of cost, from dispensaries that had been positioned along the construction line.

Quinine was at that time a commonly used medication for treating the symptoms of Malaria. However, the side-effects of the drug included temporary deafness, a condition which may have led to further accidents, as labourers on Quinine were often unable to hear the sounds that warned of danger.

The unpredictable and disease-riddled working environment also took a toll on the mental and emotional health of contracted labourers. Morale was low and there was a general feeling of despondency as individuals struggled to come to terms with the depressing reality that they were being entrapped in web of exploitation in which they were systematically overworked, maltreated and moreover, stripped of all human dignity.

The beautiful dream that was once harboured, had turned into a living nightmare.

However, the overriding mood of despondency among labourers, would have been of little or no concern to the Canal Company. The scheduled completion of the project remained the uncompromising paramount objective. Furthermore, due to the fluid availability of able-bodied young men from the Caribbean that were eager to sign-up for work on the construction, contracted labourers may have been deemed dispensable

The regular transportation of new recruits from the British colonised West Indian islands, to the Canal Zone would continue unabated throughout the process of the canal construction.

Living The Dream

During the period the canal construction, the peoples of the Caribbean had been gripped by feelings of positivity.

It was the most opportunistic time in their history and families across the social divide benefited greatly from the financial assistance they received from close family members who had been employed in various skilled and unskilled positions within the American Controlled Canal Zone.

Those from disadvantaged communities who had been resigned to a life of abject poverty, and could only dream of the better life that was seemingly beyond their reach, were being particularly emboldened. The good life, for these individuals, had at long last arrived.

They were no longer struggling with the stresses involved with day-to-day survival. For the very first time there was surplus money in their pockets which could be freely spent on purchasing the things that were required for enabling a relatively comfortable life.

Most importantly, it was no longer necessary for many children from poorer communities to attend school barefooted, as families were now able to afford the purchase of shoes, as well as items necessary for progressing their education, such as text books, note pads, rulers, and pencils.

The much-needed funds may also have been spent on placing deposits on small plots of land, purchasing materials for building, or renovating homes, and acquiring furnishings and various other home comforts.

Families from comparatively well-off neighbourhoods also benefited greatly from the additional income that was being received from loved ones employed by the American Canal Company.

It was indeed common place that at the end of each month, and across the different islands, individuals rushed to local postal offices to collect letters from bread-winners that contained the much-anticipated money order.

The ensuing "spending spree" did not only enrich living standards and by so doing, boosted the confidence of many, it also gave rise to economic growth within the region.

The general positive and inspiring upturns of the period, had been directly attributed to the cumulative large sums of "Panama money" that was being poured into the islands.

Not surprisingly, individuals who had been left on the side-lines but craved a "piece of the cake" hurried independently to the land of "milk and honey," or presented at the Canal recruitment centre in Barbados with the hope of "striking it lucky" by securing employment as contracted labourers on the canal construction.

Consequently, the availability of large numbers of men from the British Colonised Caribbean eager to take up the offer of contracted work on the building of a waterway across the isthmus of Panama, was endless.

It was overall, an unparalleled golden era for these small island nations. And a time when work opportunities loomed large, spirits were lifted, and feelings of deprivation and hopelessness had been replaced by hope and optimism of brighter days to come.

However, while dependents back home had been living their "best lives," very few had knowledge of, or could have imagined the back-breaking sacrifices that were being made, for their benefit, by loved ones who laboured on a treacherous and uncompromising jungle terrain.

Lights That Shone Through The Darkness

Even though for the most part labourers were being required to toil for at least 14 hours a day, within a harsh and disease riddled environment, there were nonetheless occasions when they were enabled the freedom to simply relax and enjoy good times.

Despite being denied work-related perks and incentives, the recruitment by the Canal Company of several hundred sex-workers from the island of Martinique in 1905, ensured that the personal desires of contracted labourers were being met. Consequently, the much appreciated "consolation prize" would have undoubtedly resulted in pleasurable moments of sexual release and subsequent feelings of rejuvenation. While, emotional comfort may have been obtained from heart-warming letters received from loved ones left behind.

By the year 1906, an estimated 24,000 West Indian labourers had been recruited. Consequently, mental strength and solace may have been derived from being participants of a workforce consisting of individuals that shared a similar background. More specifically, the general sense of togetherness that existed among labourers would have undoubtedly stemmed their collective daily experiences.

The count-down of the last few days prior to the arrival of "Pay-day" was always highly anticipated.

Labourers' wages were distributed from "pay cars." These were compartments in trains that had been specifically equipped for the very purpose.

After patiently standing in line and in turn, signing for, and collecting their hard-earned pay, labourers often headed to the post office where money orders were purchased and despatched to dependents back home.

Despite being meagrely rewarded for their laborious and risky undertakings; contracted labourers celebrated the fact that they had honoured their responsibilities and were able to jingle a few left-over coins in their pockets. Most importantly, many considered themselves "lucky" and thanked God, that they had survived to see another "Pay day."

They had miraculously dodged being seriously injured, avoided contracting one of the serious inflictions or diseases that had incapacitated or claimed the lives of so many of their fellow workers, and were therefore, deserving of some form of celebration.

The fortunate individuals would seize precious work-free moments by temporarily casting aside feelings of woe and gather in friendship groups on dirt roads adjacent to their cabins.

Meanwhile, food was being prepared in large pots and over log-fires, by various independently employed silver-roller cooks and domestic workers.

Many women from the Caribbean who were non-contract employees in hotels, restaurants, and private homes, had been alerted, by word of mouth, of the nutritional deprivations that were being experienced by contracted labourers. And whenever possible, supplemented their diet with freshly cooked meals that were wholesome and reminiscent of home.

While pots were being stirred by kindly volunteers during joyous gatherings, hearty greetings would be followed by the knocking together of bottles of cheap liquor before being swiftly downed. And as the party rolled, the drinks flowed, and large portions of freshly cooked deliciously spicey food were being devoured with relish.

These were treasured occasions when troubles were being temporarily forgotten and high-spirited merry-makers in loud voices, strived to surpass each other with humorous stories and lurid revelations of imagined or embellished sexual encounters, that were received with instantaneous roaring laughter and often accompanied by the powerful stomping feet.

The high-point of these fun-filled "get-togethers" had been the stage at which the inebriated revellers collectively belted-out slurred renditions of well-known songs of the period. And moved their bodies to the accompanying rhythms of pulsating hand-clapping and the chiming sounds of sticks beating on bottles.

At the end of the jollies, the exhilarated labourers would stagger to their cabin, slump onto their bunk-bed and immediately slip into unconsciousness.

After a short but deep and restful sleep, it was with heavy heads but rejuvenated spirits that the routine grind was resumed the following day.

Very Important Visitors

Everyone involved in the combined effort to build a waterway through the isthmus of Panama, including contracted labourers, had been awestruck when in 1906, news broke that the President of the United States, Theodore Roosevelt, accompanied by his wife, would be visiting the Canal Zone in November that very year. And it was within an atmosphere charged with excitement and giddy expectancy that the area was being cleaned, scrubbed, white-washed and essentially spruced-up in preparation for the VIP arrival.

Theodore Roosevelt who championed the building of the Panama Canal had been the first President of the United States to make an overseas diplomatic visit when he embarked on a 17-day journey to Panama and Puerto Rico on November 9th 1906. The trip was primarily taken for the purpose of carrying out an inspection of a project, which after a series of setbacks, was eventually progressing as planned.

Although yellow-fever had been largely eradicated by the year 1906, after water sources such as swamps and puddles were infused with a variety of substances that included crude oil, caustic soda and carbolic acid, other diseases such as malaria, remained prevalent. Consequently, the President was shielded from disease and the torrential rain that persisted throughout his visit by being dressed in protective clothing.

While observing operations from a slow-moving train, the president was able to witness the difficulties that were being endured by labourers on a typical working day during the rainy season. And how, with spade in hand, maintained a vigorous and energetic pattern of digging whilst being chest deep in mud and with rain continually pounding on their back.

He may also have seen the common occurrence of workers being knocked off their feet and slipping into freshly dug holes, by the force of the torrents that were being caused by sudden and unexpected landslides, and being buried beneath mountains of fast-moving earth.

Moreover, those who had been fortunate to have resurfaced relatively unscathed following the traumatic string of events, were immediately ordered to re-start what was an altogether high-risk digging process.

After fully surveying the hazardous environment in which labourers toiled, the President expressed his concerns to the Canal Company.

He suggested that appropriate measures should be taken for safeguarding the wellbeing, and improving the overall working conditions of the unskilled workers who laboured on the ground.

The Presidential investigations had been thorough and meticulous in all areas, and involved the overseeing of the work that was being carried out by different groups of operators. He rallied the workforce by expressing his appreciation for their valued contributions and urged that their motivations and collective efforts should not be allowed to falter.

President Roosevelt was passionate in conveying his firmly held belief, that participants to the unprecedented mammoth construction were on the way to being "history makers." They should therefore not waver from the path that would lead to realising the triumphant end goal.

The President's words were seen to be put into action when he fearlessly stepped onto, and took control of a large steam shovel.

Canal workers were not only captivated by the magnetic presence of their Leader and inspired by the words of encouragement that was backed by his "hands on" involvements, they could not help being charmed by his friendly and infectious toothy smile.

Despite the persistently turbulent weather, there were no postponements to the various social activities that had been scheduled for ensuring a constructive as well as an enjoyable Presidential visit. And included marching bands, lavish dinners, song and dance performances, theatrical presentations, and competitive sporting events.

At the end of what had been a productive and morale boosting tour of the Canal Zone, President Roosevelt was judged by the majority to be a likeable and fair-minded, "man of the people." And work on the construction continued with increased motivation and fervour.

Theodore Roosevelt was not destined to see for himself, the successful outcome of the construction he championed so passionately.

He would never again set foot, anywhere in the region.

Although the President's recommendations for ensuring a safer working environment for labourers remained unheeded, the men had been heartened by the unexpected appearance of a smartly dressed individual with whom they were able to identify.

The unknown but much welcomed visitor was a fresh-faced 23-year-old Jamaican born journalist known as Marcus Garvey, who was at the time and an employee of a Newspaper group that was based in the City of Colon.

Garvey was alleged to have visited the terrain at various times during the dry season in the year 1910. And appeared sympathetic to the plight of labourers as he mingled among them, conversed with some, and observed their brutal undertakings.

It is likely that the overall experience may have been profoundly impactful on his chosen future career. However, it could not have been predicted that the ambitious but unassuming young Marcus Garvey, who had taken the time to observe and interact with some of the men who laboured during the building of the Panama Canal, would some day become a world-famous Activist for Racial Justice and Equality of opportunity.

Hell's Gorge

The Culebra Cut forms part of the Panama Canal. And was the greatest and most challenging of undertakings during the process of the Canal construction.

The operation required the digging of a channel that was forty-five feet deep and 300 feet wide through an eight-mile-long mountain ridge, known as the Culebra.

Contracted labourers from the Caribbean could not have imagined the extent to which the already perilous involvements would be surpassed until they were being directed to carry-out tasks that were unsafe and highly unpredictable.

Moreover, and despite the high-risk nature of the operations, it appeared that safeguarding strategies for protecting life and limb, had not been put into place, or even considered, prior to labourers being selected at random, supplied with the necessary tools, and instructed to drill holes into mountains and fill the openings with sticks of dynamite.

Consequent to the pattern of catastrophic outcomes that were being witnessed daily, labourers were mentally prepared for the spine-chilling directives, that may have been generally received with a sense of resignation or possibly fatalism. While their spared counterparts would probably have been gripped by mixed feelings of relief and sadness.

However, "not knowing" when it would be their turn to step forward and initiate the most lethal of procedures, had been agonising for them all.

Soon after the task of boring holes into rock and clay had begun, everyone present at the work-site would flee to a place of safety and anxiously await the expected earth-shattering outcomes.

Within minutes, popping sounds were echoing and resounding across the length and breadth of terrain as rows of planted dynamite ignited in tandem.

The triggering of powerful ear-piercing smoke-emitting explosions, crumbled mountains, and resulted in particles of rock, clay, earth, and body parts being spewed high and wide into the atmosphere and showering the ground beneath.

However, due to the urgency of the operation, time was never wasted. And it was in a tensely charged atmosphere, consumed with smoke and dust. Infused with pungent odours, and the amplified sounds of groaning drills, belching steam shovels, revving engines, and roaring locomotives, that debris was being hastily scooped into steam shovels, unloaded onto trains, and speedily transported to dumping sites.

It is estimated that during a typical 14-hour working day at the Cut, the repeated cycle of lethal undertakings, amounted to six hundred holes being drilled into hard rock and filled with dynamite, several hundred lost lives and at least 160 train-loads of dumped refuse.

The excavation of a trench that was ten-stories deep in temperatures that exceeded 100 degrees Fahrenheit, or 38 degrees Celsius also resulted in fatalities that had been caused by dehydration or heat exhaustion. Moreover, common occurrences of flooding and sudden and unpredictable mud-slides during the wet season, resulted in huge numbers of labourers being swept into dug-out holes and buried alive.

Consequent to the ever-increasing number of daily fatalities, rail-road tracks were lifted and diverted to Mount Hope Cemetery, for the purpose of expediting the timely burial of bodies.

Following the heartbreaking experience of witnessing the frequent and horrific demise of friends and workmates, surviving labourers returned to their respective cabins at the end of yet another tragic and hard-working day, consumed with feelings of anguish, survivors' guilt, and despair. And with tears rolling down their cheeks, the bereft individuals would seek solace in prayer and the singing of hymns.

Due to the uncertainties that were associated with the harrowing daily dance with death, labourers would regularly pass on their treasured possessions to friends or room-mates prior to setting out on what was very likely to be their "last" day on planet earth.

This uproarious and most dangerous stage of the canal construction was known as "Hell's Gorge."

Hell's Gorge was alleged to have claimed the lives of several thousand contracted Labourers, most of whom originated from the island of Barbados.

The Finishing

Despite the unrelenting obstacles that resulted in the heavy loss of life, and the vast expenses that were being incurred, the long-held vision of a waterway across the isthmus of Panama linking the oceans of the Pacific and Atlantic remained undimmed. And was the driving force behind the mammoth undertaking, that continued unabated and at pace over a period of 10 years.

Approximately six years into the building process, significant progress was becoming visible, and by the year 1911, the almost completed construction of the Panama Canal had been making head-line news across the globe. It was at the time an exciting and unprecedented feat, and curious individuals from various countries around the world, travelled to the isthmus for the purpose of viewing what had been, back then, an unimaginable man-made endeavour.

The building of the Panama Canal was successfully completed on 10th October 1913.

The waters of the Atlantic Ocean and the Pacific Ocean were joined together by an explosion that was triggered remotely from the White House, by President Woodrow Wilson.

It had been a victorious and euphoric historical moment in time. And the small crowd of engineers and various other skilled operators who had gathered with family members for the "Grand Finale," erupted into emotional expressions of joy and relief. There were instantaneous warm embraces, congratulatory hand-shakes, jubilant cheering, and hand-clapping, and screams of delight as hats, like confetti, were being tossed in the air.

The unbridled glow that symbolised the unprecedented achievement, would radiate and shine brightly for an indefinite period, thereafter.

The official opening of the Panama Canal was formally declared by President Woodrow Wilson on August 15th 1914. The declaration was immediately followed by the passage of the American Cargo and Passenger Ship, SS Ancon.

Due to the onset of World War 1, just weeks previously on July 28th, the planned extravaganza inauguration was postponed. Moreover, the momentous event had not been featured on the front pages of the American Press.

Importantly, President Theodore Roosevelt who had championed the magnificent construction was at the time of the official opening, no longer a significant United States political figure.

After serving two full terms in Office, Roosevelt's presidency came to an end in 1909.

The completion of the Panama Canal had been a phenomenal engineering accomplishment.

The records indicate that during the building process, approximately 3.5 billion feet of earth had been excavated by 75,000 contracted labourers from the British West

Indian islands. And an estimated total of 20,000 West Indian, but largely Barbadian lives had been lost.

Although the highly acclaimed endeavour could not have been possible without the blood, sweat and steely endurance of the men from the Caribbean, many decades would pass before these unsung heroes of yester-year are officially recognized for their courage, perseverance, and indispensable contributions.

Onwards And Upwards

Following the successful completion of the Canal construction, independent economic migrants and those who had been contracted to the American Canal Company, may have juggled with the dilemma, "where do I go from here." The options were variable, they could have chosen to seek some form of alternative employment and continue to reside within the Zone. Relocate to a different province within Panama. Migrate to the United States of America, or simply return to their respective homeland.

Many of those who had taken the decision to live and work in the Canal Zone were at some point in the future, joined by spouses and/or close family members. Many families would in due course, apply for and be granted citizenship and entitlement to indefinite residency.

In the early 1920s, a significant number of new Panamanian migrants relocated on a permanent basis to areas that were near the Caribbean Sea, such as Colon and Panama City. And many went on to secure employment as plumbers, fire-fighters, policemen, carriage and trolley-car drivers, and bus conductors.

As West Indians adjusted to life in their adopted country they were being increasingly accepted within the wider community and during the late 1920s and early 1930s, were being offered plots of land, free of charge, on the outskirts of Panama City. And was for many surviving contracted labourers, a welcome opportunity for enabling fulfilment of long-held farming aspirations.

Panama was at the time a Roman Catholic, Spanish speaking nation whose culture was heavily influenced by Spanish traditions and way of life, albeit, with a sprinkling of French and North American influences. Artistic forms of expression such as music, song and rhythmic dancing had been fundamentally African inspired.

The West Indian migrant community of the era may not have been persuaded to assimilate fully into the dominate culture. But in the fullness of time, a sub-culture emerged, and was largely reflective of Caribbean norms and customs. These incorporated religious expressions, music, dance, and various other cultural traditions.

Despite becoming fluent in Spanish, the first language of British West Indian migrants had been retained.

They continued to converse with each other in their separate and unique dialect of broken English. And ensured that their children received an English education that was based on the British curriculum of the period, by establishing small independent English-Speaking schools, that were being funded by different fraternal organisations.

Similar values were at the same time, being pursued by migrants who after the completion of the canal, went on to work on banana plantations in Pacas del Tora, a North Western province of Panama. An area in which they subsequently settled and raised families.

Many of those who migrated to America may have resided in cosmopolitan areas, such as Brooklyn New York, where jobs were plentiful and opportunities for further education were easily accessible. And where different racial and cultural immigrant groups lived separately but cordially alongside each other, which was, at that time and place, the accepted norm.

Back then, Caribbeans in the United States, considered themselves fortunate to have been permitted entry into a country that was modern, and progressive, and where dreams could be realised.

These optimistic perceptions had been shared by relatives back home who may have gleefully anticipated receiving not only financial assistance from loved ones in America, but also deliveries of large packages filled with things that were for them, unavailable or unaffordable.

Among the various West Indians who benefited personally and economically after emigrating to the United States, and laid the foundation on which the generations that followed had been enabled to realise their aspirations, was Daniel Dennis Lewis.

Daniel Lewis who was born on the island of Grenada in 1897, emigrated to the United States from Panama, in 1923, at the age of 26.

He had been independently employed by the American Canal Company but following the completion of the construction, remained in Panama, and lived, and worked in Cristobal, a port town in Colon Province.

After relocating to the United States, Lewis worked as a porter for a salary of $1,200, which in those days had been considered substantial. And after securing suitable accommodation in New York City, he was joined by his wife and four children in 1924.

The family settled happily into their new environment and a fifth child arrived in 1926.

They were granted United States Citizenship in 1928.

The siblings were reported to have progressed satisfactorily at school and after graduating were successful in obtaining work positions of their choosing.

Meanwhile fond memories of the homeland were being harboured and nurtured, and the family remained financially supportive of close relatives left behind. Home was the place that Mr and Mrs Lewis planned to retire and for that reason, ensured their future by investing in property on the island of their birth.

It was however, not to be.

Daniel Lewis voluntarily enlisted into the United States Army after America entered World War 2, following the bombing of Pearl Harbour in December 1941. He was alleged to have been both proud and privileged to fight for the country which had taken him in and provided the opportunities that had transformed the lives of his family.

Shortly after the end of the World War 2, Lewis' unfortunately developed the illness that would, all too soon, claim his life.

Daniel Lewis passed away at a hospital in Manhattan, New York, in 1946, and was buried in New Jersey. He was just 49 years of age.

Many individuals who returned to their respective homeland, arrived at a period when the world was at war, and thousands of young West Indian men had been demonstrating their loyalty to the reigning King, George V, by voluntarily enlisting into the British Army.

Documents indicate that of the 15,000 West Indians who volunteered their services in World War 1, two-thirds were from the island of Jamaica.

It was also a time when the significant changes that had occurred since the beginning of the American recruitment drive in 1905, included the introduction of street lighting in towns and cities, and a relatively small number of cars and buses being driven on paved roads.

Among the returnees were those who had sustained life-changing injuries and/or were penniless. They were nonetheless, delighted to discover that apart from improving the livelihoods of loved ones, money earned in Panama had contributed towards the general financial up-turn in the economy of the colonised small island states.

It appeared that the hardships they endured and the brutal undertakings, had not been in vain.

However, despite the highly rewarding outcomes, many of those who carried out labouring tasks during the building of the Canal were mentally and emotionally scarred by their experiences. And would be psychologically burdened for the rest of their lives.

Reflections

The men who had been contracted to work as labourers during the building of the Panama Canal, and had survived the ordeal, would have undoubtedly been relieved when their services were no longer required.

They were at long last released from shackles and constrains, and in control of their lives as they transitioned to a new chapter.

Survivals who had been maimed due to serious injury, and required support as they moved forward, would have undoubtedly benefited from aids and adaptations, or artificial limbs that were being donated by various charitable organisations. Moreover, like the dependents of the deceased, injured individuals who had been deemed unfit to work, were reported to have been recipients of small monthly charitable payments.

After the initial euphoria and regardless of the country in which they had subsequently settled, one-time contracted labourers were invariably being affected by some degree of post-traumatic stress.

Those who were unable to erase haunting memories, were tormented by flashbacks of the specific catastrophic events that resulted in the demise of so many of their contemporaries. And were being plagued by restless nights and recurring alarming night-mares.

Those affected, may have deeply regretted allowing themselves to be so badly treated, but in moments of deliberation probably accepted some personal responsibility for failing to assert self-determination by simply walking away from what had been an altogether inhumane working and living environment. And a bold step that had been taken by several of their single-minded contemporaries.

Consumed by feelings of unworthiness or shame, even, the deflated souls struggled to come to terms with their deeply distressing memories of the past. However, they remained steadfast in their reluctance to burden loved ones with their "tales of woe" and instead derived mutual comfort and support from comrades with shared experiences.

This may have occurred during one-to-one encounters, or group gatherings. But these exclusive sessions would undoubtedly have been enabling to outpourings of harrowing recollections and discussion that related to their emotional and psychological difficulties.

During those meetings, individual members of the "brotherhood" may have, in turn, recounted specific painful incidents to an audience that never failed to respond with sympathetic nods or empathetic shaking of heads. However, alongside the harrowing recollections, lay a prevailing sense of disbelief that they had actually "dodged the bullet," which was being compounded by agonising feelings of survivor's guilt. But many a heartfelt tribute would be paid to the large number of friends, acquaintances, and work-mates, whose lives had been lost.

After being temporarily exorcised of their psychological demons, it was always with renewed spiritual calmness and all-round shaking of hands that the enlivened compatriots departed on their separate journey at the end of every gathering.

"See you next time" they may have chanted in friendly and up-beat tones as they headed for home.

For this wounded generation of men, any formal acknowledgement, now or in the future, regarding their crucial participation in a project that was successfully completed and widely saluted, would have been generally considered "inconceivable."

They were resigned to being labelled an undeserving species.

The Unravelling

Despite the measures that were being taken by the surviving labourers to shield relatives from having knowledge of the challenges they faced while toiling at the isthmus, the information was, in the fullness of time leaked to family members and close friends, and by "word of mouth" circulated within different communities. Furthermore, detailed information of specific horrific occurrences had been provided by those who agreed to be interviewed after being approached by various sections of the local media.

Relatives and friends of the men who had been contracted to work on the Canal construction, and the public at large were shocked and saddened by the first-hand disturbing disclosures of the men who had survived the torturous journey. Any rose-tinted assumptions that may have been harboured regarding the Panamanian experience, was at that point, comprehensively shattered.

The years marched on and those who came afterwards reaped benefits from the seeds that had been planted by the "men of courage." The plight of a long-gone generation who had sacrificed so much for enabling a flourishing future for their descendants was nonetheless never totally forgotten.

The experiences of those who had been contracted to work on the construction of the Panama Canal were being kept alive by disturbing historical accounts that were being passed down to the children and grand-children of following generations that may have resided in the Caribbean, and others who had evolved to being citizens of the United States, Panama, or elsewhere on the continent of South America.

Simultaneously, pilgrimages to Mount Hope, Gaton and Corozal cemeteries in Panama, in search of the graves of their brave ancestors were at various times being undertaken by the relatives of some of the men who perished while working on the Canal construction.

All the while, organised peaceful campaigns for obtaining official recognition for those who paid the ultimate price continued unabated. And included organised protests, the lobbying of politicians and submissions of signed petitions to the British Parliament.

One-Hundred Years Afterwards

The decades came and went, and the man-made canal across the isthmus of Panama, which had been built to connect the world by providing a cheap and quick service between the Atlantic Ocean and Pacific Ocean, proved monumentally successful.

After a period of joint American-Panamanian control, the American-led constructed artificial waterway was handed over to the Panamanian Government in 1999.

Panamanians would subsequently vote in favour of the expanding the locks, in 2006.

Time quickly marched on, and by the year 2014, Elizabeth 11, had been Queen of the United Kingdom and the Commonwealth for 62 years. Various British Colonised Caribbean islands, such as Barbados, Grenada, Jamaica, St Lucia and Trinidad and Tobago had achieved independence. And West Indians were being collectively emboldened as the islands progressed, with self-determination, into the modern world.

Meanwhile, more than 14,000 vessels and over 300 million tons of cargo were at that point passing through the Panama Canal on an annual basis. And the centre of Panama City had developed essentially into a thriving and bustling cosmopolitan area with towering skyscrapers, busy shopping precincts, gleaming restaurants and bars, museums, and a variety of glittering night-time entertainment.

Panama had also become a popular holiday destination for thousands of people from across the globe. But apart from engaging in popular activities that were available in the city, individuals may also have ventured into the country's renowned rainforests, participated in water sport, such as surfing, white water rafting or diving, or simply trekked along the jungle shores. Although exploration of the Panama Canal and its expansion, visiting the locks and boating through the waterway, may have been memorable experiences for most holiday makers.

New York Dentist, Dr Joseph Radix was one of countless individuals who had been persuaded by publicised illustrative reports and colourful videos, into embarking on a boat trip along the constructed waterway.

Dr Radix described the moment he first laid eyes on the man-made canal as being, for him, a "jaw dropping" unforgettable moment in time.

"Seeing is believing" he said, and claimed to have been particularly spell-bound and rendered speechless on seeing how the water rose, and the boats floated and were lifted into the different locks. It was, in his view, "a spectacle to behold." Radix was left in no doubt that the Panama Canal was indeed, the Eighth Wonder of the World.

Although individuals may have gasped in wonderment while viewing the motions of the water and the movements of the boats on the magnificent man-made waterway, the human sacrifices that enabled the unprecedented accomplishment, may understandably, not have entered the collective psyche.

Many descendants of surviving contracted labourers who had settled in Panama following the completion of the canal, were in 2014 residing in the Province of Colon, and at the time estimated to be around 70,000 in number.

Colon sits on the Caribbean coast at the entrance to the Canal, and near the Atlantic Ocean.

Despite being full citizens of Panama, the different Afro-Panamanian communities have retained their West Indian culture and language, and are, therefore, bilingual.

Meanwhile the descendants who had become established citizens of countries such as the United States may have achieved the fulfilling lives that had been envisaged by their fore-fathers.

However, within the various communities in which the descendants of the men who laboured on the canal construction were continuously evolving, there were those who remained steadfast in the enduring campaign for justice, while for others, the plight of their courageous ancestors may have been forgotten, or at best a distant memory.

Despite the disparity in the way different groups of descendants were being impacted, feelings of elation had been equally palpable when information of an upcoming significant event that had been one-hundred years in the making, was being circulated across the different

West Indian communities by various organisations and notable persons.

And so it was, on August 15th 2014, one-hundred years after the Official opening of the Panama Canal, a Bronze Plaque was unveiled at the Mira Flores Locks in memory of the vital participations of the men from the British West Indian Islands who paid with their lives for enabling the successful completion of the world's greatest artificial marvel.

The Plaque was financed by the British Embassy in Panama, in agreement with the Panama Canal Authority and in consultation with West Indian Community Groups.

It commemorated the 100-year anniversary of the Official opening of the Canal, and was presented by Hugo Squire, the United Kingdom Foreign Officer, Minister for Latin America.

In his address, Hugo Squire said that he was: "enormously honoured to be unveiling today a new Plaque here at the Mira Flores Locks that will memorialise the important contribution of the people of the British West Indies in the construction of the Panama Canal." He went on to express the hope that "the Plaque would be seen by all the visitors to the canal for the next 100 years."

The Ceremony was attended by organised campaigners, relatives, invited guests and sympathisers who had in some way participated in the ten-decade fight to obtain accreditation on behalf of the men who laboured on the front-line during the building of the world-famous Panama Canal.

Although an apology had not been forthcoming, the inclusion on the Plaque, of West Indians whose lives had been sacrificed during the period of the French Canal Construction, was considered a generous and therefore, most-welcome gesture of goodwill.

The unsung heroes of yester-year, would have undoubtedly been both overwhelmed and overjoyed to learn that after a duration of 100 years, barriers had been taken down and they were deservedly being posthumously awarded the long-desired prize.

The recognition they wished for but believed to be "inconceivable" had, after an extended period, transcended into actuality.

It was a victorious finale.

THE END

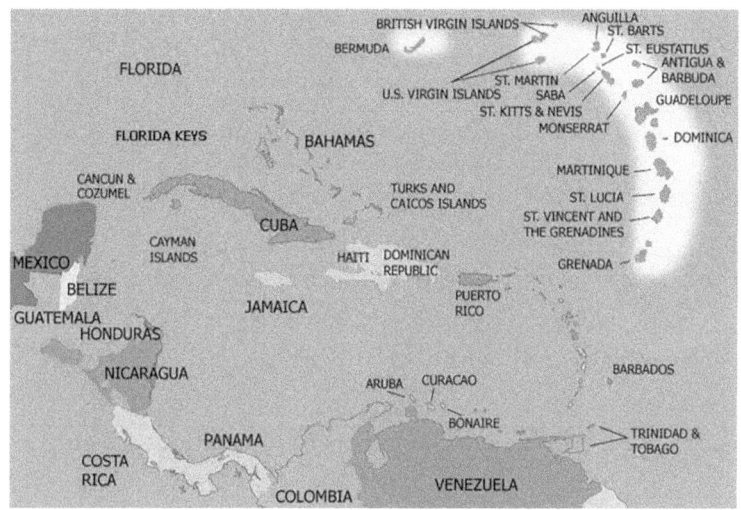

THE REGION

PANAMA

ONE HUNDRED YEARS

SILVER ROLL JOB APPLICATION

ON ROUTE TO THE ISTHMUS

NEW ARRIVALS

LABOURERS' LIVING ENVIRONMENT

LABOURERS ON THE JOB

THE PANAMA CANAL

ENTRY CERTIFICATE TO THE U.S.

LONG-AWAITED RECOGNITION OF UNSUNG HEROES

www.ingramcontent.com/pod-product-compliance
Lightning Source LLC
Chambersburg PA
CBHW041147110526
44590CB00027B/4155